BIZARRE & BEAUTIFUL FEELERS

Santa Fe Writers Group

John Muir Publications
Santa Fe, New Mexico

T 63421

Special thanks to Mary Colleen McNamara, Ph.D., Department of Biology,
Albuquerque Technical-Vocational Institute, Albuquerque, New Mexico

Santa Fe Writers Group:
Miriam Bobkoff, research
K. C. Compton
Donald E. Fineberg
Kathleen Lee
Miriam Sagan
Leda Silver

John Muir Publications, P.O. Box 613, Santa Fe, New Mexico 87504
© 1993 by John Muir Publications
All rights reserved. Published 1993
Printed in the United States of America
Printed on recycled paper

First edition. First printing September 1993
        First TWG printing September 1993

Library of Congress Cataloging-in-Publication Data
Bizarre & beautiful feelers / by the Santa Fe Writers Group.
        p. cm.
    Includes index.
    Summary: Describes the unique sense of touch of several animals,
including the scorpion, catfish, and gecko.
    ISBN 1-56261-125-9 : $14.95
    1. Touch—Juvenile literature. 2. Physiology, Comparative—Juvenile literature.
    [1. Touch. 2. Animals—Habitats and behavior.] I. Santa Fe Writers Group.
    II. Title: Bizarre and beautiful feelers.
    QP451.B59 1993
    591.1'827—dc20   93-2034
                                                            CIP
                                                            AC

Logo/Interior Design: Ken Wilson
Illustrations: Chris Brigman
Typography: Britt Gallagher
Printer: Guynes Printing Company

Distributed to the book trade by
W. W. Norton & Co., Inc.
500 Fifth Avenue
New York, New York 10110

Distributed to the education market by
The Wright Group
19201 120th Avenue NE
Bothell, WA 98011

Cover photo, Tokay Gecko, Animals Animals © Zig Leszczynki
Back cover photo, Common iguana, Animals Animals © E. R. Degginger

INtRODuctIOn

All animals on the planet, including humans, understand the world around them by using sensory organs. The senses we know the most about are sight, smell, taste, touch, and hearing. Animals use these senses to avoid predators, to find mates, food, and shelter, and to entertain themselves. Some people believe that animals, including humans, use other, less-understood senses as well. Have you ever had a "hunch" about something that proved to be true? Maybe you were using a sense other than one of the five mentioned above.

Bizarre and Beautiful Feelers is a spirited investigation into the sense of touch in the animal realm. But before we meet the twenty animals featured in this book, let's cover the basics of touch.

The walrus' long whiskers, called vibrissae, are sensitive touch organs.

The orb spider follows vibrations in its web to locate captured prey.

Walrus

Orb web spider

An Ancient Sense

Touch is perhaps the oldest sense there is. Prehistoric creatures may not have been able to see very well in the dark ocean depths, but they could feel. Even now, millions of years later, touch is the first sense humans rely on when we come into the world. When you were a baby, you felt things—such as your crib, your blanket, and your mother's hands—before your eyes could focus or sounds had any meaning. You first discovered your toes not by sight but by touch. You put small objects in your mouth not to taste them but to feel them.

Animals use their sense of touch to locate food, identify members of their family or species, move around safely in their habitat, find mates, and more. The sense of touch also helps animals, including humans, detect danger and avoid injury. Because of our sense of touch, we can experience pleasant sensations, such as stroking a pet's fur or cuddling with those we love. In fact, in many animal species "cuddling" seems to help young animals (including children) become healthy adults. Children who are held and hugged usually grow up to be happier and more confident than those who were not.

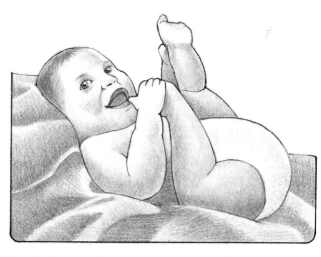

Touch is the first sense we use when we come into the world.

What Touch Tells Us

The sense of touch is sometimes divided into other senses because it covers so many types of **tactile sensation** (physical feeling). The human organs for touch, for example, can detect pressure, pain, temperature, movement, and texture, as well as more subtle sensations. We can stand outside and, from the air on our skin, tell whether it's hot, warm, cool, or cold. Some people claim they can detect tiny changes in air pressure and so can "feel" an approaching storm. We run our fingertips across a surface and immediately know if it is smooth or rough, hard or soft, wet or dry, slippery or sticky. A spider creeps up our arm and we jerk reflexively, knowing just where the creature is even though we haven't yet looked. We hold something between our thumb and forefinger and judge how thick or thin it is. We hold a rock in our hand and get a sense of its weight. We hold a feather in the other hand and feel its lightness. We sit on a tack—and yowl in pain! Our sense of touch provides all of these different kinds of information.

Our sense of touch gives us information about our environment and allows us to feel pleasant sensations.

Feelers Galore

Not all touch sense organs are alike—far from it. Mammals' touch organs are most often nerves embedded in their skin. Many insects have touch-sensitive hairs on their antennae and even all over their bodies; these are called sensilla. Believe it or not, cats and walruses have a touch organ in common: the long whiskers on their faces, called vibrissae. Other animals use their sense of touch to detect vibration. This is how the orb web spider catches its prey.

Some parts of an animal's body may be more sensitive to touch than others. The hairs between a cat's paw pads are extremely ticklish, for instance. The mole's pink nose is very sensitive and easily hurt. In humans, the fingertips, lips, nose, cheeks, and mouth are among the most sensitive body parts.

The Purpose of Pain

Aches, pains, pangs, burns, twinges, cramps—it's no fun to feel any of them. But imagine if you could feel no pain. If you grabbed a dish right out of the oven with your bare hands, you wouldn't feel a thing as it burned you. If you pulled a muscle while running, you'd just keep on moving, damaging the muscle even more. You might not even notice if you broke a bone! Fortunately, all of these things normally hurt—and trigger a reflex in you to stop whatever is causing the pain and seek help if necessary. In general, physical pain is a message that your body is under stress or has been injured and needs to heal. The pain generally goes away on its own when health is restored.

Touch Telegraph

Despite all of these different kinds of feelers, there are some common elements to the sense of touch. Cells that receive physical cues such as pressure, warmth, or pain are called **touch receptors**. Touch receptors in humans are bundles of nerves in our skin. These cells convert this information into an electrical signal and send it through the animal's nervous system to the brain. The brain then perceives (understands) the signal as touch and determines what kind of touch it is and what the animal should do in response to it.

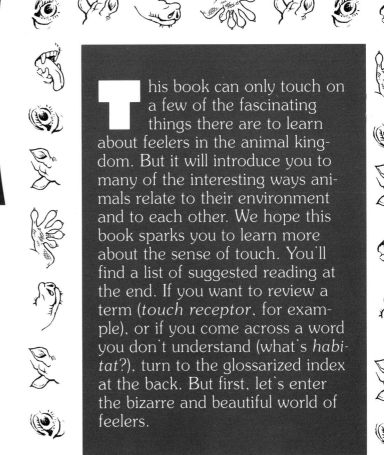

This book can only touch on a few of the fascinating things there are to learn about feelers in the animal kingdom. But it will introduce you to many of the interesting ways animals relate to their environment and to each other. We hope this book sparks you to learn more about the sense of touch. You'll find a list of suggested reading at the end. If you want to review a term (*touch receptor*, for example), or if you come across a word you don't understand (what's *habitat*?), turn to the glossarized index at the back. But first, let's enter the bizarre and beautiful world of feelers.

We're lucky we can feel pain. Lucky?! Yes. Without it we could seriously injure ourselves and not even know it.

Praying Mantis

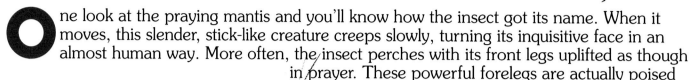

(Mantis religiosa)

Mediterranean mantis

One look at the praying mantis and you'll know how the insect got its name. When it moves, this slender, stick-like creature creeps slowly, turning its inquisitive face in an almost human way. More often, the insect perches with its front legs uplifted as though in prayer. These powerful forelegs are actually poised to snap out at unsuspecting insects that wander by. The mantis then turns its prey over and begins munching away, biting into the back of the insect's neck to sever the main nerve.

The praying mantis is an extremely successful hunter, snaring its prey a surprising 85 percent of the time. The primary tool this masterful hunter uses is its sense of touch. As it awaits its prey, the mantis is responding to information coming from hundreds of touch-sensitive hairs called sensilla. These hairs sit in a socket connected to a nerve cell. There are more than 400 hairs in each of the two hair beds on either side of the mantis' neck alone! That's not bad for an insect that measures only one to a few inches long.

The mantis always turns its head to look directly at its prey. The insect knows how far its legs should strike to capture the victim by how far its head has turned. But it has to move very fast and with great accuracy. Its big eyes aren't keen enough for the job. The praying mantis' perfect aim comes from its sense of touch, by way of the tiny hairs on its neck.

PREYING MANTIS

Praying mantises are harmless to humans, but otherwise they are fearsome fighters. The mantis itself seems afraid of nothing. It has even been known to box with kittens and to grab hummingbirds at birdfeeders! The insect's superb balance is also due to its sense of touch. Beds of sensilla located throughout the body and leg joints are stimulated as the mantis moves so it can balance on its rear quarters. From this position, it can accurately attack just about anything that moves.

The praying mantis severs the main nerve of its prey before eating it.

Praying mantis, facing page

Orb Web Spiders

(Family: Araneidae)

If you drop a line and hook into a lake to catch a fish, you won't see, hear, smell or taste the fish until you've reeled it in. You depend entirely on your sense of touch to know when you have a nibble on your line.

Spiders that build orb webs "fish" for insects in a similar way. First, the spider builds its complex web. Amazingly, this takes only about one hour. Next, the spider sits in the center of the web, head down, with its feet lightly touching the sticky lines. Then, an insect flies into the web and becomes stuck. It wriggles, trying to free itself. The web moves. Sensing these vibrations with its feet, the spider knows that dinner may be at hand. It follows the tugs on the lines to locate its victim.

Relying on the sense of touch, rather than vision or hearing, has important advantages. The web spider can hunt on a dark, moonless night as easily as in the daytime. Also, the strength of the vibration tells the spider important information about what type of prey has been caught. If the web vibrates only slightly, the spider knows its victim is small and defenseless. It races quickly to its victim, bites the tiny insect, and drags it back to its feeding area. If the web shakes wildly, the spider approaches cautiously, knowing the insect is large and could be dangerous.

Cobwebs that gather in the corners of rooms and behind furniture are webs left behind by spiders who moved on or died. But most spiders don't just leave their old haunts: they eat them before respinning a new one.

AVOIDING THE TRAP

Did you ever wonder how a spider avoids getting caught in its own trap—the sticky web? It's as easy as one-two-three! First, the spider keeps its body off of the sticky, silken threads. Second, it has special claws at the end of its legs that only lightly touch the web's threads. And third, it secretes a special oil on its legs so the threads of the web won't stick to them.

The orb web spider locates prey by following the vibrations the trapped insect makes when it struggles.

Orb-weaving spider, above and facing page

Grasshoppers

Short-horned grasshopper

At small airports you can see a wind sock fluttering in the breeze on top of the control tower. Pilots check the wind sock to see from which direction and how strong the wind is blowing. For a safe take-off, airplanes need to propel down the runway into the wind.

Grasshoppers take off all the time. But they don't use a propeller to get airborne: their large hind legs launch them. For a successful lift-off, they too must propel themselves into the wind. But how does the insect know which way the wind blows? Its sense of touch tells it.

A grasshopper may look like it's covered with green armor, but this crusty shell is actually covered with many fine, touch-sensitive hairs called sensilla. Five different groups of sensilla grow on the grasshopper's head alone. If the air around the hopper's head moves only slightly, the sensilla can detect it. In fact, scientists measured a reaction in a grasshopper when its sensilla was moved less than a millionth of a foot! When the sensilla move, they stimulate nerve cells that send signals to the grasshopper's brain. The brain then determines if the direction and velocity (speed) of the wind are right for take-off.

The types of sensilla on the hopper's body serve different purposes. Some act as an alarm if another creature tries to grab the insect. Some alert the hopper when dirt or debris strikes its body. These sensilla trigger a grooming response.

WHY SO MANY SENSILLA?

Scientists remain puzzled as to why grasshoppers are covered with so many types of touch receptors. There are many sensilla on the hopper's underside. Do these tell the insect to elevate its belly so it won't get stuck to a sticky leaf? There are also sensilla on the inside of the insect's legs; these are called the Brummer's organ. When the hopper is still, this organ rests against the side of its body. Does this have something to do with the instinct to hop? There is a lot we don't understand about grasshoppers.

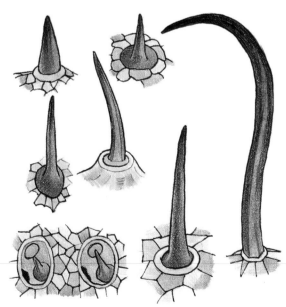

The grasshopper's body is covered with different types of touch-sensitive hairs called sensilla.

Venezuelan grasshopper, facing page

Sand Scorpions

(Order: Scorpionida)

This interesting creature has poor vision. It doesn't smell the insects it feeds on. And it doesn't hear them either. How does it manage to find its prey? Touch-sensitive hairs on its eight legs accurately sense the vibrations insects make when they move in the sand. These hairs are called—you guessed it—sensilla.

Sand scorpions live in the hot, dry Mojave Desert, where temperatures soar to over 150° degrees F (70° C) in the middle of a summer day. Nighttime is the right time for hunting if you're a sand scorpion. In the relative cool of the evening, the scorpion emerges from its underground burrow to perch on the sand. It sits very still, sometimes waiting for several hours for a moth, insect, or even a smaller sand scorpion to wander by. When it hunts, the scorpion relies on the sensilla on its eight legs to detect information about the presence and location of a possible meal. When prey ventures near, the scorpion opens its pedipalps (prey-capturing pincers), extends them forward, and raises its body off the sand. It stays motionless when the prey is still. But each time the insect moves even slightly, the scorpion creeps closer. At last, it snatches its prey! The scorpion then paralyzes it with a poisonous sting from the end of its tail.

Scorpions are arachnids, like their eight-legged cousins the spider, mite, and tick. They can reach a length of 3 inches (about 8 centimeters) and, if undisturbed, live for five or six years. Their stings can be fatal even to large animals and humans. You know what else? Some sand scorpions appear flourescent under ultraviolet light—they glow in the dark.

TIME TO LAY LOW

Sometimes a scorpion has bad luck in hunting. If it has been a long time since its last meal, the scorpion can "turn down" its metabolism. (Metabolism is the rate at which an animal uses its energy.) Then it stays inactive inside its burrow and can survive in this semi-dormant state for several weeks or even a few months.

The sensilla on the scorpion's eight legs detect the movement of prey in the sand.

Tail and stinger of African emperor scorpion, facing page

TIger SWallowtAils

(Papilio glaucus)

In the world of butterflies, the tiger swallowtail is a long-distance flier. With its small, lightweight body and large wings, the swallowtail rides the air currents great distances seldom beating its wings. How does it do this? It is very sensitive to changes in air pressure and then to the air currents that these changes create.

The butterfly's nervous system consists of a brain and two nerve cords that run through the body. Small numbers of nerve cells along these cords branch out to all parts of the swallowtail's body. On the butterfly's wings are bristly sensilla (touch-sensitive hairs) that are extremely sensitive to air pressure changes. As the butterfly flies through the air, these bristles tell it where to catch the best gusts of wind on which to glide.

The butterfly's antennae are also amazingly responsive sense organs. They handle the insect's senses of balance and smell. The base of each antenna houses a special organ, called the Johnston's organ, that helps maintain the butterfly's orientation during flight. (Orientation is "getting your bearings," knowing where you are in relation to your surroundings.) Without the Johnston's organ, the butterfly might fly upside down or even in circles!

Butterflies have three pairs of legs, and their sense of touch is important here as well. Sensory cells around the leg joints tell the butterfly how to bend its legs and move its body.

AIRY VEINS

If you look closely at a butterfly's wings, you will see a delicate network of veins. Unlike human veins, which carry life-giving blood, the butterfly's veins contain mainly air. This network of air-filled veins makes the butterfly's wings float like soap bubbles. Over the veins is a layer of colored scales that gives each kind of butterfly its special markings—and that's a lot of markings. There are more than 20,000 species throughout the world. The tiger swallowtail got its name from the yellow or orange and brownish stripes that cover its wings.

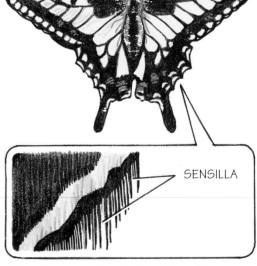

SENSILLA

The tiger swallowtail seldom flaps its wings when it flies. The touch-sensitive bristles on its wings tell the butterfly where to catch gusts of wind on which to glide.

Tiger swallowtail butterfly, above and facing page

Trap-Door Spiders

(Family: Ctenizidae)

Trap-door spiders don't weave webs. They live in holes in the ground that they cover with a hinged lid made of spun spider silk. This lid resembles a trap door. When night comes, the trap-door spider pokes its head and front legs out of the opening of its covered burrow. It sits and waits for its next meal to walk or wriggle by.

Any small, passing bug will do. The spider cannot see its prey well in the dark. Crawling bugs do not make much noise. The spider cannot smell them. How does it know that the passing beetle or grasshopper or ant is within reach? The spider's legs, which stretch out from under the trap door, are covered with fine hair. If a passing beetle brushes against these hairs ever so slightly, the spider seizes the unsuspecting insect with its front legs. With its back legs, the spiders anchors itself in its house, and then drags the victim under the trap door.

Another kind of trap-door spider covers its burrow opening with a leaf. When an insect crawls across or lands on the leaf, the leaf vibrates. The spider feels the vibration with its sensitive hairs, which brush against the bottom of the leaf. It then rushes out of the burrow and snares its prey. Still other kinds of trap-door spiders spin "trip wires" of silk in front of their burrows. If an insect stumbles across one, the vibration alerts the spider and it lunges out to attack its prey.

THE NOD OF DEATH

After a trap-door spider drags its prey into its burrow, it raises its head and bites its victim. Why does it give its dinner this little nod? Unlike most spiders, which have fangs that close from each side like pincers, trap-door spiders have jaws similar to ours, with fangs on the top and bottom. When the trap-door spider opens its jaws to bite its victim, it looks like it's nodding its head.

The trap-door spider lies concealed in its burrow. If a passing insect brushes against the fine hairs on its outstretched legs, the spider seizes the unsuspecting animal.

Trap-door spider, above and facing page

16

Fiddler Crabs

(Uca minax)

Touch is the most important sense to fiddler crabs. It helps them forage for food, detect enemies, find mates, and avoid obstacles. Their amazing tactile ability even helps them maintain their balance. Bristles and hairs are the secret to the crabs' powerful sense of touch. Touch receptor bristles grow all over the crab's body. Most are on the walking legs, especially at the ends.

Hairs on the crab's claws can sense how hard or soft an object is when the crab pinches it. Other specialized hairs, called thread hairs and free hook hairs, allow the crab to detect the direction and strength of water currents as they flow against the crab's body. Other hairs are sensitive to low-frequency vibrations caused by the movement of things nearby. A submerged fiddler crab, for example, will react to a single drop of water falling on the surface over its head.

Despite their name, you won't find fiddler crabs making music. They got their name from their appearance. The male has one very large claw that often is as big as the rest of his entire body. The crab holds this large claw close to his body—and looks like he's playing the fiddle!

Fiddler crabs are small creatures, only about 1 inch (2.5 centimeters) long. They live together in great numbers on tropical sandy beaches. They dig into the sand between the tide lines and come out to feed on microscopic plants and animals when the tide goes out. Females use both claws for feeding. But males can use only their smaller claw. When the tide comes in, all fiddler crabs hide in their individual burrows in the sand.

Fiddler crab claw

WARNING! NO TRESPASSING

Fiddler crabs stridulate. That is, they make a shrill sound like crickets and grasshoppers do. They do this by rubbing a small spike on their elbow against a row of teeth on the edge of their shell. If a crab tries to enter a burrow that's already occupied, the crab inside stridulates. The would-be visitor gets the message and scoots away.

Only male fiddler crabs have one very large claw. The claws of female fiddlers are about the same size.

Male fiddler crab, facing page

CatFish

(Genus: *Ictalurus*)

European catfish

As a rule, catfish live mainly on the bottoms of lakes. Here, the water is brown and murky, and it is difficult to see. But the catfish has unique whiskers that let it feel for food. These whiskers are called barbels, and each catfish has three or four sensitive pairs. When the catfish swims near the lake bottom, it holds its barbels down so they glide over the bottom, feeling for a possible meal.

European catfish live in rivers as well as deep lakes. They may spend the day in the mud, using their barbels to feel for small invertebrates (animals without backbones). But it is at night that the catfish becomes truly active, hungrily feeding on frogs, fish, and crustaceans. (Crustaceans are aquatic animals with segmented bodies and shells, such as lobster, crabs, and shrimp.) The Brown catfish eats mostly worms and other animals without a hard shell. Since they also hunt at night and have poor eyesight, they rely solely on the sense of touch to find their prey. Catfish are so blind that a worm can pass right in front of them and they won't notice. But the instant that worm touches a whisker, the catfish snaps up the creature.

Some marine catfish have poisonous spines, and in the tropics there are parasitic catfish that attach themselves to other fish, or even to human beings. But as a rule, catfish are gentle, simply using their feelers to sort through the mud and brackish water for dinner.

TOUCHY-FEELY FISH

The catfish is not the only fish that is sensitive to touch. The blind cave fish has nerves along the sides of its head that are super-sensitive to touch. The same is true of piper fish, mottled sculpins, and other fish that hunt at night. These nerves together are called the lateral line organ. These organs help the fish detect the tiny plankton it feeds on, as well as sense obstacles ahead. Subtle changes in the water flowing over the its body tell the fish to change course to avoid a collision. In some fish, lateral line organs run down both sides of the whole body.

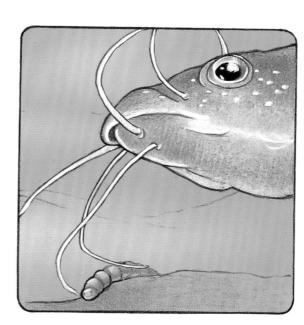

The catfish finds food using its sensitive whiskers, called barbels.

Tiger shovel-nosed catfish, facing page

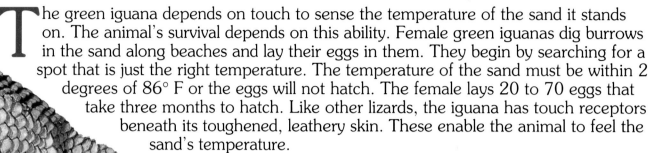

GREEn IGUAnas

(Family: Iguanidae)

The green iguana depends on touch to sense the temperature of the sand it stands on. The animal's survival depends on this ability. Female green iguanas dig burrows in the sand along beaches and lay their eggs in them. They begin by searching for a spot that is just the right temperature. The temperature of the sand must be within 2 degrees of 86° F or the eggs will not hatch. The female lays 20 to 70 eggs that take three months to hatch. Like other lizards, the iguana has touch receptors beneath its toughened, leathery skin. These enable the animal to feel the sand's temperature.

Green iguanas look very awkward with their heavy tails and wide legs. In fact, they are remarkably agile and can scramble easily from one tree to another on connecting branches. All creatures that move about with great agility depend on a highly developed sense of touch. Without the many touch receptors in the skin of their feet, stomach, and tail, the iguana would be clumsy. Imagine how difficult it would be to walk if you couldn't feel the ground with your feet. The iguana could never scurry about if it could not feel where the branches, twigs, and rocks are.

These lizards cannot leap far, but an iguana 50 feet up in tree will take the short way down: it throws itself to the ground and, without a scratch, quickly scurries off. Iguanas are vegetarians and eat many parts of plants, including flowers, leaves, and fruit. Some young iguanas eat insects. Iguanas are hunted by snakes, human beings, and hawks. In many parts of the world they are considered to be a delicious food.

Front foot of iguana

LIFE AS AN IGUANA

Green iguanas have a combed crest down their backs and are a pale green color. They live in trees in tropical forests and are fond of water. When in danger, the green iguana often will escape to water. They can swim under-water, using their tails to propel them along. They prefer to live in trees over-hanging pools or rivers. They come down to the ground only when it's cold to hide beneath logs or in holes.

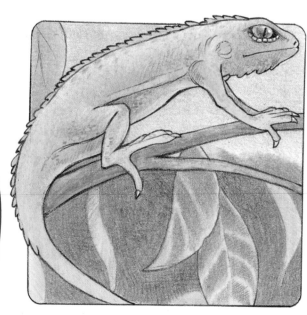

Its keen sense of touch helps the iguana scurry with ease from tree to tree.

Common iguana, facing page

Mallards

(Anas platyrhynchos)

A duck's bill is hard, like a bone or a shell. Yet it is one of the most sensitive parts of the bird's body. Rows of touch receptors clustered together line the edge of a duck's bill. This feature is especially important to dabbling ducks such as the mallard. Dabblers upend themselves (turn upside down and dive) to forage on the muddy bottom of the lake or river in which they live. They use their sensitive bills to poke around for something good to eat. When ducks dabble, their rear ends stick straight up out of the water. Mallards also feed on the surface of the water and from the mud on the banks.

If a duck is dabbling in water instead of mud, its sensitive tongue gets in on the action. It acts like a straw to suck water into the duck's mouth and then push it out, leaving only edible particles behind. Filters along the edges of the bill let out objects the duck is not interested in eating. Mallards can feed either during the day or night since they don't need sight to forage. They eat leaves, seeds, grains, berries, insects, and small fish.

A duck's webbed feet are also highly sensitive to touch. They may waddle awkwardly, but ducks actually pick their way carefully through sticks and pebbles on the shore or bank. They step on round, smooth objects and steer clear of sharp sticks and rocks. The duck is using its sense of touch to keep its balance and to avoid hurting its feet.

P.S. The wild mallard is the ancestor of most domesticated duck breeds.

FEATHER FEELERS

There are touch receptor cells in the mallard's feathers, in both their long contour feathers and in their short bristling feathers. The receptors in the bristle feathers send messages to the duck's brain about the location of the contour feathers. These cells help the duck arrange its feathers, clean them, and position them properly when flying.

Mallards use their sensitive bills to search for food in the muddy bottoms of lakes and rivers.

Mallard drake (male), above and facing page

Sloths

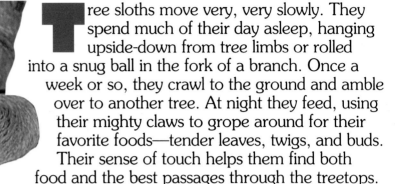

(Genus: *Bradypus*)

Tree sloths move very, very slowly. They spend much of their day asleep, hanging upside-down from tree limbs or rolled into a snug ball in the fork of a branch. Once a week or so, they crawl to the ground and amble over to another tree. At night they feed, using their mighty claws to grope around for their favorite foods—tender leaves, twigs, and buds. Their sense of touch helps them find both food and the best passages through the treetops. Their hearing and sight are poor.

Sloths can turn their necks and forearms all the way around to three-quarters of a complete circle. Their front limbs are much stronger and more flexible than the hind ones. The animal can roll its body into a perfect ball, so that its nose touches the top of its tail. Most sloths have a curve in their lower back, just enough to make up for the difference in length between their hind and front legs.

Three-toed sloth

Two-toed sloth? Three-toed sloth? Neither species can move its digits (fingers or toes) independently. They are fused together. If the animal wishes to move to another place in the tree, it uses a slow hand-over-hand motion. Even when perched snugly in the fork of a tree, the sloth's claws are securely hooked to a branch. What if they must defend themselves? Tree sloths can slash quickly and inflict deep wounds. They can also use their teeth in defense. Generally, when left alone, they are gentle creatures. But they are no match for the chainsaw. Sloths are endangered by loss of habitat (living space) because the South American forests in which they live are being cut down.

GREEN HAIR

Imagine moving so slowly that things started to grow on you. Such is the case with the tree sloth. Green algae often grow on these arboreal (tree-dwelling) animals during the wet seasons. These tiny plants live close to the surface of the sloth's crisp, straw-like hairs and give a green tint to its grayish-brown fur.

The sloth spends most of its time hanging upside-down in trees. When it gets hungry, it gropes for tender leaves and buds with its powerful, sensitive claws.

Three-toed sloth's claw, facing page

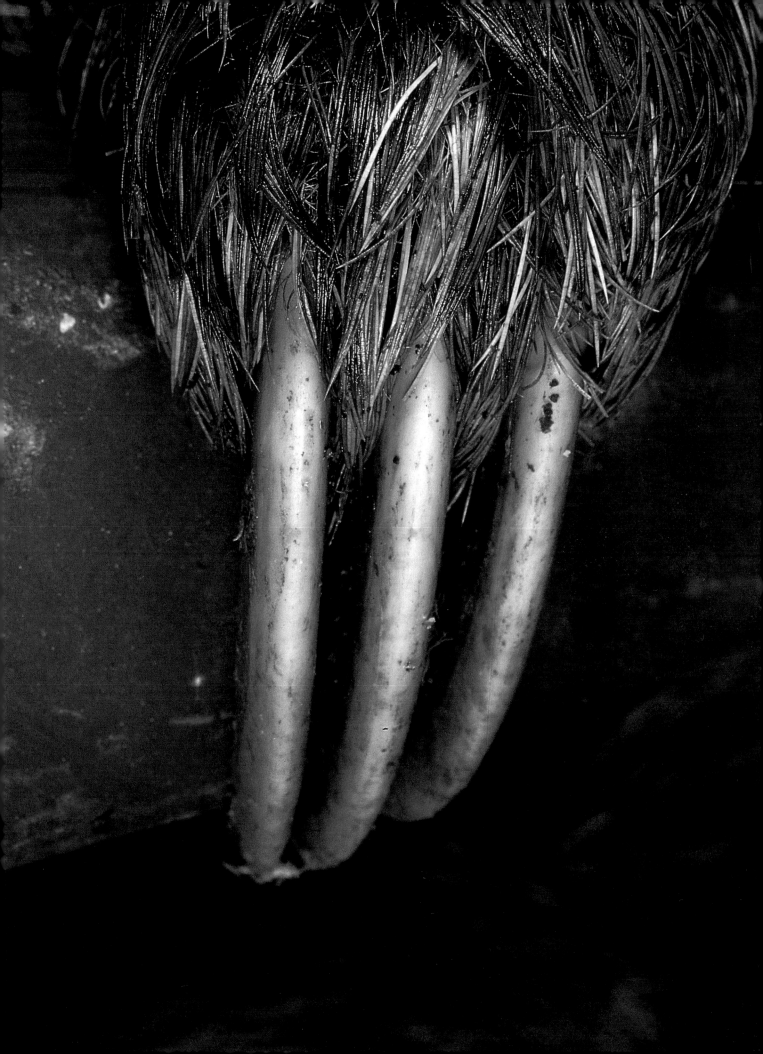

MORAY EELs

(Family: Muraenidae)

There are 100 species of morays that range in length from 6 inches to 10 feet. If you came eye to eye with a moray of any size, you'd probably get quite a scare! They have sharp fang-like teeth set in a forceful jaw, thick skin without scales, and a body that looks like a snake's. In fact, they are usually very shy and dart back into their holes when large creatures pass by. They have been known to attack, however, when they are cornered or taunted.

The eel is perfectly adapted to life in a reef. Since their heads are shaped like wedges and their bodies are smooth and muscular, they can easily squeeze in and out of nooks and crannies in the rocks. Eels have every reason to stay close to home in both reef and rock. It is here that they can best find the crustaceans and small fish that make up the bulk of their diet. And when eels are not out hunting, crevices make an excellent place to hide from predators.

An unusual reflex helps the eel navigate and hide itself in these tight spaces. This reflex prompts the eel to automatically reorient its body whenever it brushes against a wall of rock or coral. If its tail dangles outside of a crevice, for example, the eel reflexively pulls back inside for protection. This reflex is also found in other reef inhabitants, such as fish that lurk in rock cracks. Special sensory pits that look like dots decorate the faces of some moray eels. These pits sense vibrations in the water and help the eel detect creatures moving nearby.

THE FRIENDLY EEL

Can you imagine petting a moray eel? They may not be the cuddliest of creatures, but some divers have made friends with them. If a moray gets to know a diver who feeds it a fish now and then, the moray may behave like a tame animal. Some will even sit in a diver's hands. But if the diver moves too quickly or jerks the food away, the alarmed moray may bite the hand that feeds it.

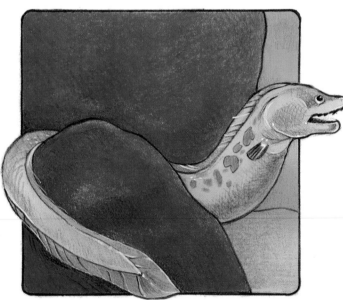

The moray eel's keen sense of touch helps it navigate through narrow passages in its reef habitat.

Spotted moray eels, facing page

CATS

(Family: Felidae)

Domestic cat

Cats purr when they're petted and rub up against you when you stop, as if asking for more. Cats like to be touched because it feels good to them. How does a cat feel through the fur covering its body? Many of the strands of hair on a cat's body are rooted directly into sensitive touch receptor cells. When the cat's hair is touched, these receptors alert the cat's brain, which interprets the touch. Some hairs on a cat have a high number and variety of touch receptors. They are sensitive to even the slightest breeze. Other cat hairs require brisk brushing before the cat notices.

The next time you see a cat stalking a mouse, a bird, or a grasshopper, pay special attention to its whiskers. When a cat springs at its prey, its whiskers shoot forward as far as possible. Once the prey is captured, the whiskers curve around the prey to keep track of its movements. A cat's whiskers are densely packed with touch receptors. Even before they are touched, the whiskers can detect the vibrations of nearby movement. Cats also use their whiskers to navigate in the dark. Feeling with its whiskers, a cat easily pads about in a pitch black room, avoiding collisions with walls and objects. Cats' whiskers can also keep them out of too-tight spots. If its whiskers don't easily clear the entrance to an enclosure or passage, the cat will stay out of it.

P.S. The technical term for cat whiskers is vibrissae.

TICKLISH KITTY

Have you ever lightly tickled the hair between a cat's paw pads? The cat will twitch its leg and finally lift its head, hoping you'll leave it alone. A cat's paw pads and the hairs between them are very sensitive to touch. The area on its front legs above the cat's wrist is also thick with a patch of very sensitive hairs. These hairs act like the whiskers, sensing objects not yet touched but close to the paws.

Cats curve their whiskers around captured prey to keep track of its movements.

Siberian tiger, facing page

30

M o L es

(Genus: *Scaptonyx*)

Moles spend most of their lives digging in underground tunnels in search of food. They need to eat almost constantly and, in fact, may die if they go without food for even 12 hours. Their favorites are worms and underground insects. Working both day and night, they forage tirelessly for these creatures in their dark world. Moles have tiny, weak eyes, and some are completely blind.

The mole's sense of touch, however, is very keen. The animal's hairless pink snout is covered with thousands of tiny touch sensors called Eimer's organs. Special sensory hairs called vibrissae cover the mole's skin. The mole becomes very alert when its vibrissae detect vibrations. The direction, strength, speed, and duration of these vibrations tell the animal whether there is an insect nearby—food—or possible danger. Working together, the Eimer's organs and vibrissae give the mole an incredibly powerful sense of touch.

Most moles have short tails that are covered with sensory hairs. The mole often holds its tail up so it brushes against the walls and roof of the tunnel. The tail can sense vibrations passing through the soil. But the tail can be more than just a warning system. The star-nosed mole of North America stores fat in its long tail for extra energy during mating season.

Moles are pests to gardeners because they're champion diggers. But there's a sure-fire way to repel them. Push empty bottles into the mole burrows with the necks sticking out of the ground. When the wind blows, it makes a hollow, piping sound in the bottles. The vibrations from this noise will travel into the mole's burrow and drive these super-sensitive creatures away.

Mole paw

VELVETY SOFT

Most moles have very soft fur. The hairs are all about the same length and will lie in any direction, like velvet. The features of its fur allow the mole to go backwards and forwards with ease in tight burrows. In contrast, many other mammals dislike having their fur rubbed "the wrong way." Stroke a cat from its tail up to its head, for instance, and it will probably flick its tail in annoyance or even stalk away.

The mole's tail brushes against the walls and roof of the burrow to sense vibrations.

Common mole, facing page

Crocodiles

(Genus: *Crocodylus*)

American crocodile

The crocodile's thick, scaly skin is like armor. But despite their hard, bumpy skin, crocodiles are sensitive to touch and seem to enjoy being touched by other crocodiles. Touch receptors are clustered beneath their scales. There are heavy concentrations of these receptors around their heads and necks, so these parts of a crocodile are especially sensitive to touch. Crocodiles often rub snouts and necks with each other, especially before mating. It may be their way of shaking hands, hugging, or just checking each other out.

Crocodiles are reptiles, and reptiles are cold-blooded, which means they can't maintain a constant body temperature like we do. They can't shiver to stay warm or sweat to cool down. But they are still sensitive to hot and cold temperatures, and they like to stay comfortable. When they're cold, they bask in the sun. They retreat to the shade when they're warm. At night, they sleep in the water because it holds heat longer than air does.

When a crocodile is in the water it lays low, only poking its eyes and bulging nostrils above the surface. To hold this position, crocodiles carry several pounds of rocks in their stomach to weigh them down. Otherwise, the natural buoyancy of their lungs would make them float on the surface. In this position, a crocodile can fool other creatures: its thick, bumpy skin looks like an innocent log floating in the water.

CROCODILE TEARS

Crocodiles live in warm rivers and wetlands in Africa, Asia, Australia, and America. Most crocodiles eat a variety of food, including insects, spiders, frogs, fish, snakes, small mammals, and smaller crocodiles. Very large crocodiles—some reach a length of more than 20 feet (7 meters)—also eat large mammals and have been known to attack humans. More than half of the 21 species of crocodiles are endangered because humans hunt them to make shoes, belts, and purses out of their skin.

Crocodiles have many touch receptors around their heads and necks. They often rub necks and snouts with each other.

Crocodile skin, facing page

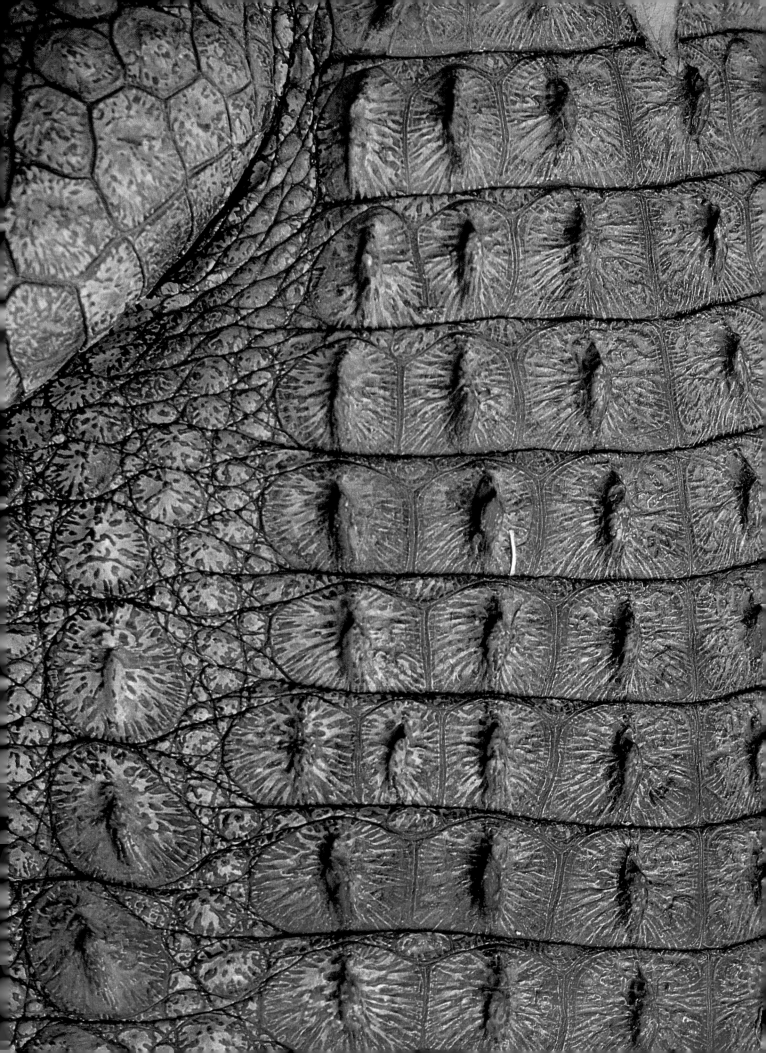

Platypuses

(*Ornithorhynchus anatinus*)

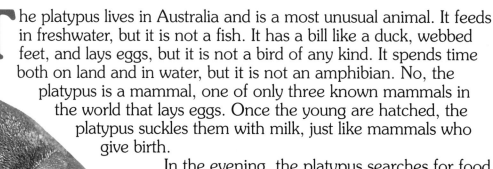

The platypus lives in Australia and is a most unusual animal. It feeds in freshwater, but it is not a fish. It has a bill like a duck, webbed feet, and lays eggs, but it is not a bird of any kind. It spends time both on land and in water, but it is not an amphibian. No, the platypus is a mammal, one of only three known mammals in the world that lays eggs. Once the young are hatched, the platypus suckles them with milk, just like mammals who give birth.

In the evening, the platypus searches for food at the bottom of its lake or pond. When it dives, it plugs its nose and holds its breath—for up to a minute—and closes its eyes and ears to protect them from the muddy water. So how does the platypus find its food? It stirs up the rocky bottom with its bill in search of things that wriggle and squirm, such as worms, larvae, or shrimp.

If you were to reach your hand into the mud at the bottom of a pond, the 20,000 or so touch sensors in your skin would tell you when your fingers touched a rock or a worm. But the platypus' bill, sometimes called its snout, has almost fifty times more touch sensors than your hand does—nearly a million! Some of these sensors on the platypus' bill measure temperature. Others detect texture and movement.

A FEEL FOR LAND AND SEA

Take a close look at the feet of the platypus. They have claws like many other mammals but also webs between them like a duck. These feet are built for life both in water and on land. In the water, the platypus spreads its claws and the webs serve as flippers. On land, the platypus pulls its toes together and its claws stick out to give it a firm grip on the slippery mud. The platypus also uses its claws for digging a burrow, the hole in the ground where it lives and lays its eggs.

The platypus scoops up mud at the bottom of the river with its bill to find worms, larvae, and shrimp.

Platypus, above and facing page

36

GEckos

(Family: Gekkonidae)

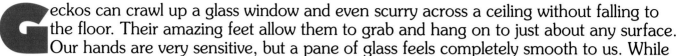

Geckos can crawl up a glass window and even scurry across a ceiling without falling to the floor. Their amazing feet allow them to grab and hang on to just about any surface. Our hands are very sensitive, but a pane of glass feels completely smooth to us. While we can feel the bumps and ridges in the texture of a wall, we couldn't climb it without a rope or a ladder. What gives geckos such a powerful foothold? It used to be thought that geckos had suction cups on the bottom of their broad flat toes, or that the bottom of their feet were covered with a very sticky substance. Actually, their strange-looking feet are covered with thousands of hooks so small they can only be seen with a microscope. To run across the glass in a window, the gecko finds tiny footholds in the surface of the glass that we cannot feel or even see. With lightning speed, the lizard slips its tiny hooks into these minuscule holes and ridges. Then it reaches forward with another foot, hooks onto more holes and ridges, and releases its grasp on the previous ones. The hooks on a single toe can support many times the weight of an average gecko. The ability to climb on just about any surface allows geckos to catch insects from the underside of tree limbs or in the high corners in houses.

Tokay gecko toes

LONG-LIVED LIZARD

Geckos have been around for a long, long time. In fact, they are one of the most ancient animals on Earth. These nocturnal lizards live in warm climates. (Nocturnal means active at night.) They are beneficial to humans because they eat insects that bother us or can even harm us: mosquitoes, flies, ants, and many others. Some geckos live in houses and eat the insects that gather around electric lights. Geckos have large prominent eyes that help them see at night. They have no eyelids and instead moisten their eyes by licking them with their long tongues.

Geckos can scurry across a ceiling without falling to the floor because the bottom of their feet are covered by many tiny hooks that grab the surface.

Tokay gecko, facing page

38

WALRUSES

(Genus: *Odobenus*)

Junenile walrus

If you're a walrus, every meal is at the bottom of the sea. These animals dive to the ocean floor for food, often staying underwater for up to 10 minutes at a time. Then they swim back to the surface for air. Even though they spend a lot of time in the water, walruses are mammals and so need air to survive.

Almost all of their prey live on or even beneath the sediment that covers the ocean floor. They sense their prey by touch, using their tusks (which are like huge, curved teeth) and their vibrissae. Vibrissae? Yes. Vibrissae are the large facial hairs on the walrus' snout and above its eyes that look like whiskers. But they are more than just whiskers. The walrus uses its vibrissae to dig through the sediment to find its food. The vibrissae grow longer and thicker as the walrus ages.

The walrus eats mostly mollusks, small shellfish. But they don't eat the shell. They suck the animal out of its home and leave the shell behind. They can eat thousands of mollusks in a single day.

Sometimes food is scarce, and walruses must try even harder to probe for their next meal. Scientists have found furrows and shallow pits in the sea bottom where walruses went "rooting" for prey. That can leave a lasting impression on the ocean bottom.

These animals are white or light gray in color. They almost always travel in small groups. Sometimes they gather together in herds of up to several thousand.

ICE IS NICE

Walruses live mostly on floating ice over shallow waters of the North American continental shelf. They prefer ice for resting, mating, and bearing young. If no ice is handy, they'll go to the land—usually small, rocky islands. They lounge close together, often with the youngsters lying on top of the adults. The baby calf stays with its mother at least two years, sometimes longer if no younger sibling is born.

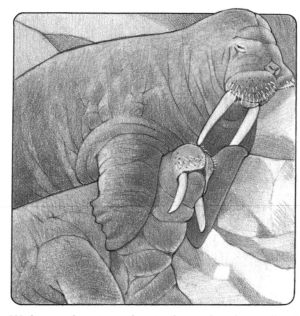

Walruses live together in large herds on floating ice. They lie close to one another.

Walrus, facing page

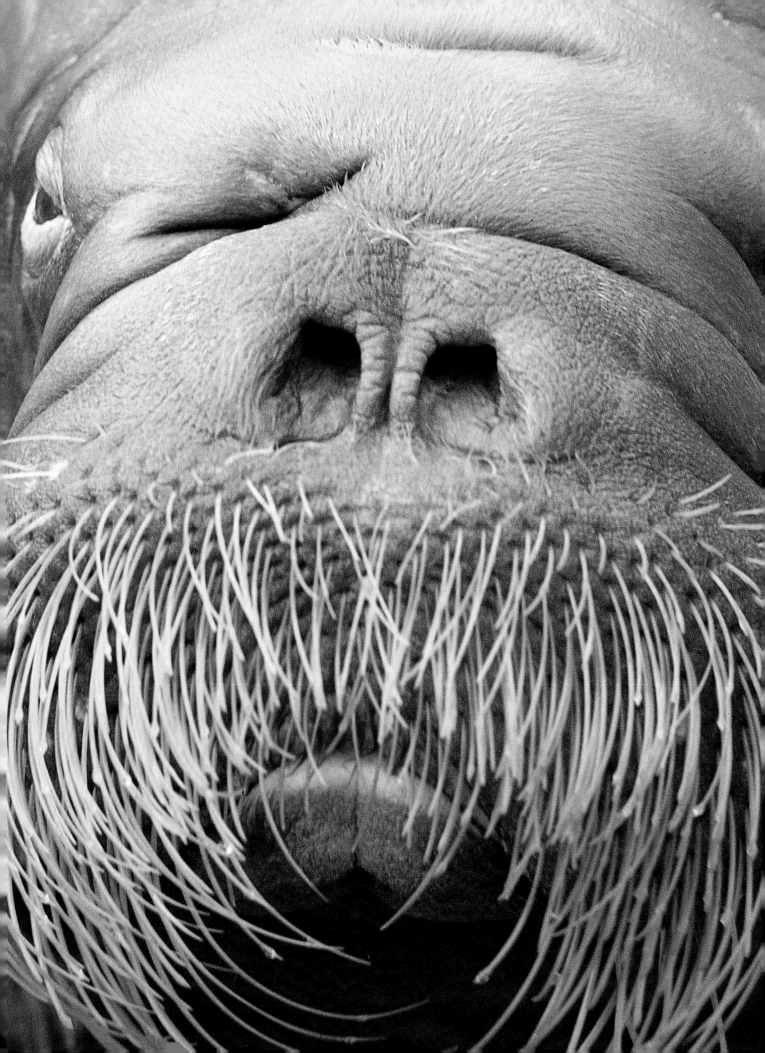

ORANGUTANs

(Genus: *Pongo*)

Orangutans, like humans, are primates. They have long arms and strong, hook-shaped hands and feet. They climb or swing between trees in the tropical forests with great ease, aided by their big grasping thumbs. They never let go of one branch until they have a solid grip on another. These large apes have a high number of touch receptors in the skin of their hands and feet. Much of the orangutan's brain is devoted to processing information from these touch receptors.

Orangutans need to eat a lot of food. Sometimes they will munch steadily for an entire day. Fruit makes up more than half of their entire diet. They especially love mangoes, figs, jackfruit, and durians. Their sensitive hands are very useful in gathering fruit because they often explore parts of trees that are hidden from sight. They use only their fingers, not their whole hand, to squeeze fruit to see if it's ripe, just like humans do. Orangutans also eat tender leaves, insects, bark, eggs, and squirrels. They drink water from tree holes, using their hands to gather the water. They slurp the liquid as it dribbles down their hairy wrists.

Orangutans also have touch receptors in strands of their hair. But the soles of their feet and the palms of their hands are the most sensitive areas, and the most useful to them.

RED-HEADED ISLANDERS

Orangutans are large, red-haired apes that live in the jungles of Borneo and Sumatra, Southeast Asian islands. Adult males are about 4.5 feet (1.4 meters) tall and weigh 150 pounds (68 kilograms). They are arboreal (tree-dwelling) creatures and rarely spend time on the ground. They eat an enormous amount of food, mostly fruit, and their sensitive touch enables them to select ripe fruit from high branches out of their view. They are mostly solitary creatures and live long lives. Because of increased logging in their forests, the range of their habitat has decreased substantially in recent years.

Orangutans grope with their sensitive hands for food they can't see.

Adult male orangutan, facing page

HUMANS

(Homo sapiens)

We experience touch in many different ways. You have special touch receptors that detect pressure on your skin. Some are tiny nerve endings; they react to very light pressure. Others, right under the surface of your skin, feel the texture of the object that you touch. With your eyes closed, you can feel the difference between a woolly sweater, a silk shirt, or a metal spoon. You can tell them apart because each of these objects has a different texture.

Have you ever jumped when a spider crawled up your arm or leg? You didn't see the creeping bug, but you knew it was there. Your skin receptors detected its movement. Your sensitivity to light touch is improved by the hairs on your body. Each hair has its own small nerve ending similar to the sensilla on other creatures. Try touching a single hair on your arm with the point of a pencil. You can feel it because your hair nerve endings are very sensitive.

When your classmate pokes you with a finger, you know what happened. Pressure receptors far below your skin measure the strength of the touch. You can tell in an instant whether the poke was a friendly way to get your attention or an unfriendly attempt to hurt you. Other receptors in your skin tell you whether something is hot or cold.

HOW TO SCRATCH A MOSQUITO BITE

When a pesky mosquito lands on your arm, you can slap it without seeing it. Your skin helps to locate it exactly. When you feel a touch, the skin does two things. It sends a signal to your brain, and it stops the skin right next to it from sending its signal. This is called inhibition. If you miss the mosquito and it bites you, the bite will start to itch. If you scratch it, the bite will swell up and may become infected. Instead, scratch a circle around it. Each piece of skin in the circle sends a "touch" message to the brain and it reduces (or inhibits) the "itch" message from the bite. Soon the bite will heal and the itch will go away by itself.

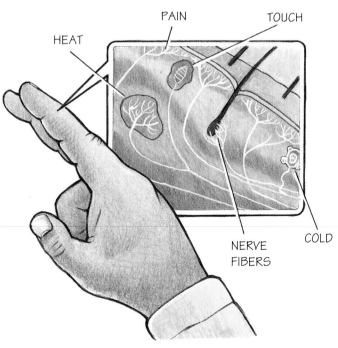

Different touch receptors in our skin detect texture, pressure, movement, and temperature.

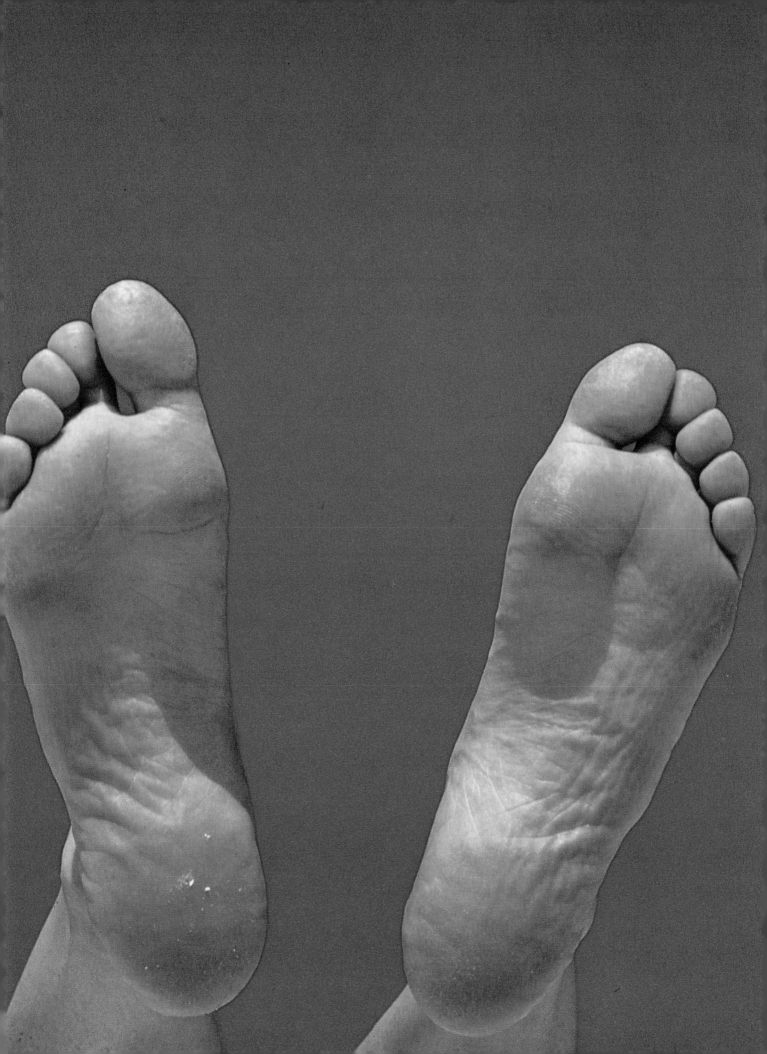

GLOSSARIZED INDEX

This glossarized index will help you find specific information about the sense of touch. It will also help you understand the meaning of some of the words used in this book.

agility—the ability to move quickly and easily

antenna—one of a pair of thin, sensitive projections on the heads of many insects and some crustaceans that carry the organs for hearing, touch, and smell, 5, 6, 10, 14

antennae—plural of **antenna**

barbel—whisker-like organ of touch made of bone and cartilage; the catfish has three or four pairs of barbels, 5, 20

butterfly, 14

catfish, 20

cat, 30

centimeter—unit of measurement in metric system, equal to 0.4 inches

crocodile, 34

crustacean—aquatic animal with a segmented body and a hard shell, such as the lobster, crab, and shrimp

domesticated—tamed; in the service of humans, such as cattle and sheep

dormant—in a state of rest or inactivity, 12

duck, 24

endangered—faced with the threat of extinction, or dying out, 26, 34

family—third-narrowest category of **taxonomy**

feelers—organs that detect tactile sensation; in insects and some crustaceans, these are **antennae**, 5

fiddler crab, 18

fish, 20

forage—to search for and gather food

gecko, 38

genus—second-narrowest category of **taxonomy**

grasshopper, 10

habitat—an animal's natural environment; living space

human, 44

iguana, 22

insects, 6, 10, 14

invertebrate—an animal without a backbone, such as mollusks and **crustaceans**

Johnston's organ—organ at the base of some insects' antennae that helps the animal maintain its balance and orientation, 14

kilogram—unit of measurement in metric system, equal to 2.2 pounds

lateral line organ—touch-sensitive organ in some fish that runs the length of the body, 20

mallard, 24

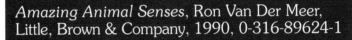

Other books about animals and the five senses:

Amazing Animal Senses, Ron Van Der Meer, Little, Brown & Company, 1990, 0-316-89624-1

Animal Senses, Jim Flegg, Newington Press, 1991, 1-878137-21-2

Extraordinary Eyes: How Animals See the World, Sandra Sinclair, R.R. Bowker, 1991, 0-8037-0806-8

Fingers & Feelers, Henry Pluckrose, Watts, Franklin, Incorporated, 1990, 0-531-14050-4

Tongues & Tasters, Henry Pluckrose, Watts, Franklin, Incorporated, 1990, 0-531-14049-0

Touch, Taste & Smell, Steve Parker, Watts, Franklin, Incorporated, 1989, 0-531-10655-1

Why Do Cats' Eyes Glow in the Dark?: (And Other Questions Kids Ask about Animals), Joanne Settel & Nancy Baggett, Atheneum-MacMillan, 1988, 0-689-31267-9

Photo credits:

pg. 3:
(walrus) Animals Animals © Johnny Johnson
(orb web spider) Animals Animals © K. G. Preston-Mafham

pg. 6:
Animals Animals © M. A. Chappell

pg. 7:
Animals Animals © Zig Leszczynski

pg. 8:
Animals Animals © Raymond A. Mendez

pg. 9:
Animals Animals © J. A. L. Cooke/Oxford Scientific Films

pg. 10:
Animals Animals © Stephen Dalton

pg. 11:
Animals Animals © Stephen Dalton

pg. 12
Animals Animals © Arthur Gloor

pg. 13:
Animals Animals © Zig Leszczynski

pg. 14:
Animals Animals © Bruce M. Wellman

pg. 15:
Animals Animals © E. R. Degginger

pg. 16:
Animals Animals © Sean Morris

pg. 17:
Animals Animals © E. R. Degginger

pg. 18:
Animals Animals © Zig Leszczynski

pg. 19:
Animals Animals © Joe McDonald

pg. 20:
Animals Animals © Zig Leszczynski

pg. 21:
Animals Animals © Miriam Austerman

pg. 22:
Animals Animals © Patti Murray

pg. 23:
Animals Animals © E. R. Degginger

pg. 24:
Animals Animals © Margot Conte

pg. 25:
Animals Animals © Robert Maier

pg. 26:
Animals Animals © Aldo Brando

pg. 27:
Photo Researchers, Inc. © Dr. Paul A. Zahl

pg. 28:
Animals Animals © W. Gregory Brown

pg. 29:
Animals Animals © Michael Pitts/Oxford Scientific Films

pg. 30:
Photo Researchers, Inc. © Jeanne White, Ottawa

pg. 31:
Animals Animals © John Chellman

pg. 32:
Animals Animals © Tony Tilford/Oxford Scientific Films

pg. 33:
Animals Animals © Leonard Lee Rue III

pg. 34:
Animals Animals © Zig Leszczynski

pg. 35:
Animals Animals © G. I. Bernard/Oxford Scientific Films

pg. 36:
Photo Researchers, Inc. © Tom McHugh

pg. 37:
Animals Animals © Hans and Judy Beste

pg. 38:
Animals Animals © Breck P. Kent

pg. 39:
Animals Animals © E. R. Degginger

pg. 40:
Animals Animals © Zig Leszczynski

pg. 41:
Animals Animals © Frank Sladek

pg. 42:
Animals Animals © John Chellman

pg. 43:
Animals Animals © Joe McDonald

pg. 44:
Photo Researchers, Inc. © Dick Luria

pg. 45:
Photo Researchers, Inc. © Art Stein

EXTREMELY WEIRD SERIES

All of the titles are written by Sarah Lovett, 8½" x 11", 48 pages, $9.95 paperback, $14.95 hardcover, with color photographs and illustrations.

Extremely Weird Bats
Extremely Weird Birds
Extremely Weird Endangered Species
Extremely Weird Fishes
Extremely Weird Frogs
Extremely Weird Insects
Extremely Weird Mammals
Extremely Weird Micro Monsters
Extremely Weird Primates
Extremely Weird Reptiles
Extremely Weird Sea Creatures
Extremely Weird Snakes
Extremely Weird Spiders

X-RAY VISION SERIES

Each title in the series is 8½" x 11", 48 pages, $9.95 paperback, with color photographs and illustrations, and written by Ron Schultz.

Looking Inside the Brain
Looking Inside Cartoon Animation
Looking Inside Caves and Caverns
Looking Inside Sports Aerodynamics
Looking Inside Sunken Treasure
Looking Inside Telescopes and the Night Sky

THE KIDDING AROUND TRAVEL GUIDES

All of the titles listed below are 64 pages and $9.95 paperbacks, except for *Kidding Around the National Parks* and *Kidding Around Spain*, which are 108 pages and $12.95 paperbacks.

Kidding Around Atlanta
Kidding Around Boston, 2nd ed.
Kidding Around Chicago, 2nd ed.
Kidding Around the Hawaiian Islands
Kidding Around London
Kidding Around Los Angeles
Kidding Around the National Parks
  of the Southwest
Kidding Around New York City, 2nd ed.
Kidding Around Paris
Kidding Around Philadelphia
Kidding Around San Diego
Kidding Around San Francisco
Kidding Around Santa Fe
Kidding Around Seattle
Kidding Around Spain
Kidding Around Washington, D.C., 2nd ed.

MASTERS OF MOTION SERIES

Each title in the series is 10¼" x 9", 48 pages, $9.95 paperback, with color photographs and illustrations.

How to Drive an Indy Race Car
  David Rubel
How to Fly a 747
  Tim Paulson
How to Fly the Space Shuttle
  Russell Shorto

THE KIDS EXPLORE SERIES

Each title is written by kids for kids by the Westridge Young Writers Workshop, 7" x 9", and $9.95 paperback, with photographs and illustrations by the kids.

Kids Explore America's Hispanic Heritage
112 pages

Kids Explore America's African American Heritage 128 pages

Kids Explore the Gifts of Children with Special Needs 128 pages

Kids Explore America's Japanese American Heritage 144 pages

ENVIRONMENTAL TITLES

Habitats: *Where the Wild Things Live*
Randi Hacker and Jackie Kaufman
8½" x 11", 48 pages, color illustrations, $9.95 paper

The Indian Way: *Learning to Communicate with Mother Earth*
Gary McLain
7" x 9", 114 pages, two-color illustrations, $9.95 paper

Rads, Ergs, and Cheeseburgers: *The Kids' Guide to Energy and the Environment*
Bill Yanda
7" x 9", 108 pages, two-color illustrations, $13.95 paper

The Kids' Environment Book: *What's Awry and Why*
Anne Pedersen
7" x 9", 192 pages, two-color illustrations, $13.95 paper

BIZARRE & BEAUTIFUL SERIES

A spirited and fun investigation of the mysteries of the five senses in the animal kingdom.

Each title in the series is 8½" x 11", $9.95 paperback, $14.95 hardcover, with color photographs and illustrations throughout.

Bizarre & Beautiful Ears
Bizarre & Beautiful Eyes
Bizarre & Beautiful Feelers
Bizarre & Beautiful Noses
Bizarre & Beautiful Tongues

RAINBOW WARRIOR SERIES

What is a Rainbow Warrior Artist? It is a person who strives to live in harmony with the Earth and all living creatures, and who tries to better the world while living his or her life in a creative way.

Each title is written by Reavis Moore with a foreword by LeVar Burton, and is 8½" x 11", 48 pages, $14.95 hardcover, with color photographs and illustrations.

Native Artists of Africa
Native Artists of North America
Native Artists of Europe

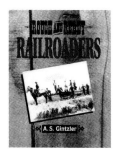

ROUGH AND READY SERIES

Learn about the men and women who settled the American West. Explore the myths and legends about these courageous individuals and learn about the environmental, cultural, and economic legacies they left to us.

Each title in the series is written by A. S. Gintzler and is 48 pages, 8½" x 11", $12.95 hardcover, with two-color illustrations and duotone archival photographs.

Rough and Ready Cowboys
Rough and Ready Homesteaders
Rough and Ready Loggers

Rough and Ready Outlaws & Lawmen
Rough and Ready Prospectors
Rough and Ready Railroaders

AMERICAN ORIGINS SERIES

Many of us are the third and fourth generation of our families to live in America. Learn what our great-great-grandparents experienced when they arrived here and how much of our lives are still intertwined with theirs.

Each title is 48 pages, 8½" x 11", $12.95 hardcover, with two-color illustrations and duotone archival photographs.

Tracing Our English Roots
Tracing Our French Roots
Tracing Our German Roots
Tracing Our Irish Roots

Tracing Our Italian Roots
Tracing Our Japanese Roots
Tracing Our Jewish Roots
Tracing Our Polish Roots